To

_____

_____

From

_____

_____

Date

_____

Dear Gui:

This book is dedicated to you, and to all the children in the world.

Your great-great-grandmother wrote it when your great-grandmother was a child, like you, and was about to receive her First Communion. She wanted her daughter to know the meaning of "The Imitation of Christ", a beautiful book written in Latin by the friar Thomas ã Kempis over five hundred years ago.

I was also privileged to have had this companion in my childhood. It helped me to understand what the Child Jesus expected from me to be good and happy.

I hope you will keep this book as your companion, and allow its teaching to help you grow like a beautiful flower – a good and faithful Christian – in Child Jesus' garden.

With love,

Grandma Thaïs

The Imitation of Child Jesus

A child's reading
of "The Imitation of Christ"

Book II

My Inward Child Jesus and Me

My Best and Everlasting Friend
at All Times

Chapter I

Child Jesus
Child, talk to Me whenever you feel sad.

Child's Heart
I want to hear what my Child Jesus has to say to me. Happy is the child who knows how to hear the Word of Child Jesus inside her heart! Oh! Heart of mine, forget earthly amusements, and listen to Child Jesus.

Child Jesus
I am your best friend! Just stay by Me.

Child's Heart
What is Child Jesus saying to me?

_____

_____

_____

Chapter II

Child's Heart

My Sweet Child Jesus, my heart wishes nothing else than hearing Your voice because all You say is wise and truthful.

I know Your 10 Commandments by heart, so help me to follow them so I can grow up as a good Christian.

The 10 Commandments are subsumed in two:

_____

_____

_____

Chapter III

Child Jesus
Listen, My dear little lamb: I am your little Shepherd, and I am calling you.

Child's Heart
The Saints say that the one who will hear the voice of the Lord shall not be unprotected on Earth.

Child Jesus
Come to me, My child, I am your best friend! There are many children that have to go on long walks to play at a friend's house; but there are many that need only one step to approach Me.

Child's Heart
My Child Jesus, teach me to fulfill Your wish. I can hear Child Jesus calling me when…

_____

_____

_____

Chapter IV

Child Jesus
Dear child, find Me and speak out the truth, tell Me all that is in your little heart.

Child's Heart
My Child Jesus, only Your advice makes me happy, I want to listen to You.

Child Jesus
I am the truth! Repent of your mistakes, child. It depends only on you to be good. It is not enough to speak about Me. You must take Me into your heart. Do all the good you can, and always look for Me.

Child's Heart
I can feel Child Jesus helping me to…

_____

_____

_____

Chapter V

Child's Heart

Child Jesus, I thank You for remembering me. When I am with You, my heart is filled with joy, as nothing is sweeter than Your great love. Whoever loves Child Jesus is filled with happiness that cannot be removed.

My heart is filled with joy when…

_____

_____

_____

Chapter VI

Child Jesus
You still do not love Me enough, child.

Child's Heart
Why do You say so, Child Jesus?

Child Jesus
I say so because sometimes you give up on Me as soon as you are upset. The evil angel is always expecting you to forget My Commandments and My Saints, because he is only happy if he can drive you to wrongdoings, and he would even make you stop having Communion if he could, because this is how it is. Remember, whenever he tries to give you bad thoughts, just think of Me and tell him strongly: Go away, bad angel, for my Child Jesus, my God, is with me.

Child's Heart
I show that I love Child Jesus more, when I…

_____

_____

_____

Chapter VII

Child Jesus
Be devoted child, but do not boast about your devotion. Be humble at heart and resistant to the world's unfairness.

Child's Heart
I am humble when I…

_____

_____

_____

Chapter VIII

Child's Heart

I don't deserve Your great kindness. I have received much ingratitude from many friends. Help me forgive them and love and serve only You, my Child Jesus.

I forgave a friend when…

_____

_____

_____

Chapter IX

Child Jesus

If you want to be happy child, accept Me as your Master. Remember that all the blessings that you will receive shall come from Me, because I am the Spring of Good. If you and your friends are good, just remember that you could have achieved nothing without Me.

Child's Heart
With the help of Child Jesus, I achieved…

_____

_____

_____

Chapter X

Child's Heart

I will approach the Nativity of Bethlehem and will say to Child Jesus: You are my King and my Lord. I owe You all. You are the infinite kindness. I am nothing. I love You, and I wish to devote my life out of gratitude for Your holy kindness.

I reflect Child Jesus' holy kindness when I…

_____

_____

_____

Chapter XI

Child Jesus
Dear child, I want to teach you many good things that you still do not know.

Child's Heart
What is it that I still don't know, my Sweet Child Jesus?

Child Jesus
That you shall only follow My Commandments and wishes. Whenever you want anything, try to see if it would please Me or not. Do not follow things because they appear to be good, and do not reject them if at first they appear to be bad. Find out about intentions, be moderate even in your devotions, but be firm if necessary on resisting temptations.

Child's Heart
I resist a temptation when I…

_____

_____

_____

Chapter XII

Child's Heart
Child Jesus, I can already tell that it is a world of struggles and hardship.

Child Jesus
It is so, My child. There is much struggle, but happy are the ones that know how to struggle with courage. And where can you find this courage? Only in My love! Was your teacher unfair to you? Send for Me, and you will find comfort. Did your friend betray you? Look for Me, and you will find consolation.

Child's Heart
I found comfort in Jesus' love when…

_____

_____

_____

Chapter XIII

Child Jesus
Obey and you will make Me happy. Your greatest enemy may be yourself if you do not know how to control your whims. Do not judge yourself better than others, be humble. Look at Me, I am the King of Heaven and Earth, but do you find Me on a regal throne? No! In a barn! Be humble and obey!

Child's Heart
My heart suffers the fear of offending Child Jesus. My Sweet Jesus, give me the desire to obey You.

I obey Jesus when I…

_____

_____

_____

Chapter XIV

Child Jesus
Dear child, I want you to say: "Child Jesus, if it is Your wish, then I want it to be done. If it pleases You then what I desire will happen. But if You see that something is not good for me, help me to do Your will always!"

Child's Heart
I please Child Jesus when I wish for…

_____

_____

_____

Chapter XV

Child's Heart

I can only find happiness and sympathy in Child Jesus. Who else than Him to understand me and comfort me in my inner hardships? Heart of Child Jesus – source of consolation!

I feel comforted and understood when…

_____

_____

_____

Chapter XVI

Child Jesus
Let Me guide you, child. You are like a little blind person that will not go a step further without your cane, and your cane is My wisdom – lean on it.

Child's Heart
Yes, Child Jesus, the blind who won't lean on Your cane shall fall.

I need Child Jesus to guide me when…

_____

_____

_____

Chapter XVII

Child Jesus
You must be agreeable and as ready for disappointment as you are for happiness.

Child's Heart
Child Jesus, I promise to be agreeable and ready for disappointment for the sake of Your love when…

_____

_____

_____

Chapter XVIII

Child Jesus
Child, I came down to Earth to save you. I became a child like you to teach you to be patient about the frustrations of earthly life. My childhood was one of suffering, struggle, and pain. I was stalked by the evil King Herod, who wanted to kill Me, and I suffered for the little ones that were killed during the search for Me. Did you know about that, child? Do not ever forget it.

Child's Heart
Child Jesus, if You suffered so much to save me, and to follow the wishes of Your Father, I am willing to suffer in Your name when…

_____

_____

_____

Chapter XIX

Child Jesus
What bothers you, My child? Are you sad? Did anyone speak badly of you? Any unfairness? Be patient – I shall be with you!

Child's Heart
Strengthen my heart, my dear Child Jesus. You know I am weak and that I hesitate at the least obstacle. Child Jesus makes me feel strong when…

_____

_____

_____

Chapter XX

Child's Heart
Child Jesus, balm of sad hearts, have mercy on me! I confess my weakness – make me strong!

Child Jesus
Here I am, child! You called Me and I came. You called Me from the heart, so I am here!

Child's Heart
Child Jesus comes to me whenever I call Him. I am ashamed for not calling Child Jesus more often. I am calling You now for…

_____

_____

_____

Chapter XXI

Child's Heart

Guide me, my Child Jesus, so I shall never boast about my good actions for which I thank You with a humble heart. But I will write here a good deed that I did recently:

_____

_____

_____

Chapter XXII

Child Jesus
Child, I will teach you the way of peace! You must follow the advice of the wise. Do what is good for others before doing what is good for you. Be happy with little. Avoid bad company and disorder. Ask God to fulfill His divine wishes, and in this way, you shall find peace!

Child's Heart
I must behave in this way, because I feel that whenever I stray from these teachings, I lose my inner peace. Child Jesus, please release me from the bad thoughts, words. and actions, and enlighten my reasoning.

I only want to have good thoughts like these:

_____

_____

_____

Chapter XXIII

Child Jesus
Child, do not be too nosy. Why do you need to find out about other people's lives? What does it matter if someone walks, speaks, or behaves in a certain way? Avoid being nosy, critical, and a bully. Take care of yourself!

Child's Heart
I will not mock and bully my friends when…

_____

_____

_____

Chapter XXIV

Child Jesus
I came to the world to bring peace. Everyone desires peace, but very few know how to find it.

Child's Heart
What shall I do, Child Jesus?

Child Jesus
Always have in mind pleasing Me in whatever you do. Do not judge your friends or strangers. Do not judge yourself better because you received something you wanted, and do not believe you deserve My love more than your neighbor just because you seem to be more devoted to Me.

Child's Heart
I will no longer think that I am better than…

_____

_____

_____

Chapter XXV

Child Jesus
Love Me dear child – I am your Savior. Fulfill your chores, do your homework without expecting rewards – love Me, and your prize will be that My heart will be yours.

Child's Heart
My Child Jesus, the love of Your name shall make me care less for games, TV, candies and beautiful clothes, so I will have time to pray and adore You.

_____

_____

_____

Chapter XXVI

Child Jesus
Do you know what a conscience is? I will explain it to you: conscience is the state of the soul before God. Whenever you do well, your soul will be at peace before God, but if otherwise, you will do evil; your soul will not be able to stand before the Creator. If anyone speaks badly of you, it will not matter because your conscience is at peace. Let those who gossip say whatever they want about you. Just be good and you will find peace in your little heart.

Child's Heart
I feel anxious and don't know how to calm down. My Child Jesus, please come and help me. Only You can bring peace to my heart. I need help with…

_____

_____

_____

Chapter XXVII

Child Jesus
Quiet down My child, as I am always right here with you, even when you think that you are away from Me.

Child's Heart
I feel Jesus closer to me when I…

_____

_____

_____

Chapter XXVIII

Child Jesus
Child, listen to My advice: "Leave all and you shall find all." Do not think of yourself; forget your vain wishes, and only wish for My heart.

Child's Heart
I must despise earthly riches. Child Jesus was born in a barn, and some animals kept Him warm with their breathing. To help the poor children in the winter I will…

_____

_____

_____

Chapter XXIX

Child Jesus
Child, you are fine today. Talk to Me. However, do not believe that what is good in your life today will last forever; tomorrow may be different. So do not ever be away from Me. Only with Me will you have the strength to resist the temptations of the evil angel that never sleeps!

Child's Heart
I understand the evil temptations now. Here are three of them:

_____

_____

_____

Chapter XXX

Child Jesus
Child, beware of the evil angel that is always trying to find the means to tempt you. My Saints were also tempted and suffered anxieties, but they knew how to overcome with patience and faith.

Child's Heart
"Love God above all" is the First Commandment. My Child Jesus, please make me follow this Commandment always, so I will not fall into temptation. I want to write down three things that I need to be patient:

_____

_____

_____

Chapter XXXI

Child Jesus
Child, do not worry about what your friends or acquaintances think of you when you are doing good. Defend yourself if necessary, but forget about them. I know what is in your little heart.

Child's Heart
Jesus, I will try not to be angry when my friend…

_____

_____

_____

Chapter XXXII

Child Jesus
There are children that look for Me in times of anxiety, and once calmed down, they forget about Me. You must always come to Me, even in your happiness, because I want to know of all the good that is going on with you.

Child's Heart
Some of the good things that are in my heart are:

_____

_____

_____

Chapter XXXIII

Child Jesus
Dear child, are you in danger? Are you very sad and worried? Only in My heart will you find comfort and strength.

Child's Heart
Child Jesus, today You gave me the strength to…

_____

_____

_____

Chapter XXXIV

Child Jesus
When you ask Me to give you something, make sure that it is indeed what you want. How many times do you want something and then, when you get it, you no longer want it? Think first, and only then ask.

Child's Heart
I will ask You to help me to be an obedient good child and become better in:

_____

_____

_____

Chapter XXXV

Child Jesus
My child, if your neighbor is popular and you are despised, please do not be sad; think of Me in Heaven, and you will forget about the earthly unfairness. Remember child: you will only find peace in My heart.

Child's Heart
Child Jesus, I have not loved You as You deserve. This may be why some have despised me. Please make me deserve Your love.

_____

_____

_____

Chapter XXXVI

Child Jesus
You must study religion, child. Learn what is in your books, and ask Me for explanations of whatever you do not understand. However, do not go so deep into the Divine Mysteries that no man can explain them to you. Some have learned about the Divine Mysteries by loving Me, but only a few…

Child's Heart
I need to understand…

_____

_____

_____

Chapter XXXVII

Child Jesus
Whenever something does not please you, just close your eyes and try to find Me deep in your heart. Only in Me will you find your well-being.

Child's Heart
I will close my eyes when…

_____

_____

_____

Chapter XXXVIII

Child Jesus
Child, did you hear bad words? Do not worry about them – your ears got hurt, but not your soul.

Child's Heart
I have searched in vain for sympathy among some people. Only in Your heart, my Child Jesus, can I hide my sadness. Some people may lie, but Child Jesus only speaks the truth. When you were only 12, you silenced the rabbis. I believe in You, my Sweet Jesus. You comfort me when I…

_____

_____

_____

Chapter XXXIX

Child Jesus
Do not worry if you are unhappy today, as tomorrow you will be happy again. You can trust Me.

Child's Heart
How happy I feel just by contemplating a picture of the Nativity! I adore my little Infant Jesus smiling in the manger. Blessed are the shepherds that adored Him and that played lullabies with their flutes for His divine sleep. Next Christmas I will…

_____

_____

_____

Chapter XL

Child Jesus
Whenever you want to come to Me and feel that this wish was inspired from Heaven, do not hesitate, child. Come look for Me. If you go out, you want to wear the clothes you like best. In the same way, when you come to see Me, dress up your little soul with the purest white veil of sincerity.

Child's Heart
My Child Jesus, there are times when I feel very happy, but some other times I feel anxious, and sometimes I don't know exactly why. I put myself in Your merciful hands. Please support me to…

_____

_____

_____

Chapter XLI

Child Jesus
Child, you can not live always in constant devotion. You belong to the world and must live in it where you have your tasks. Do your homework, do your chores, assist the unhappy, and help your parents and others whenever you can.

Child's Heart
My Lord, You are extremely kind, my Sweet Child Jesus. I always find in You a comforting voice and an everlasting forgiving heart that waits for me. I want to be better when doing the following chores:

_____

_____

_____

Chapter XLII

Child Jesus
Dear child, do not complain of too many chores and work. Do not be too curious or mischievous. Do not search the beautiful nor be sad with unfairness. Neither boast for being pampered nor pamper the rich and powerful. Your nature is subjected to it all, but just ask for the Divine Grace and you will find tranquility in your heart.

Child's Heart
Sweet Child Jesus, so often I feel my courage and the desire to please You weakened. Give me Your Grace as a light to brighten the darkness I am in. I will be strong when…

_____

_____

_____

Chapter XLIII

Child Jesus
Child, you have to choose between two roads to follow in life. I am the Way of Truth – of Good. If you follow Me, you will find sweet and eternal happiness. Follow Me, Child! You now know My Commandments and wishes – just follow them and I shall be always with you.

Child's Heart
Sweet Child Jesus, I want to imitate You, to follow Your example of humbleness. I promise to be humble when…

_____

_____

_____

Chapter XLIV

Child Jesus
Child, do not give up just because you made a mistake. Repent from deep in your heart, and I shall forgive you. Tomorrow you may fall again, but always come back to Me and you shall find forgiveness.

Child's Heart
Child Jesus, I want to commit to be better as…

_____

_____

_____

Chapter XLV

Child Jesus
Child, do not ever forget this: believe in the Mystery that the Church teaches you, but do not try to unveil it. Accept Divine Justice, and do not try to find out why some are happy and others are unhappy. You shall never be able to understand My justice, for men's intelligence is worth nothing before God's wisdom.

Child's Heart
Child Jesus, I shall only trust You, as only You are the straight road that I must always walk by.

Charity – I find charity, where I hide my repentance and sadness, in Your kind heart.
Hope – I find hope that gives me strength to live in Your sweet smile.
Faith – I find faith that brightens my future in the glowing light of Your eyes.

My Notes

My Notes

My Commitments

My Pictures

Place your photo here

My Pictures

Place your photo here

Place your photo here

My Pictures

Place your photo here

Place your photo here

Place your photo here

Copyright © 2004 Thaïs Lips
Cover design copyright © 2015 Thaïs Lips
Cover design file created using Cover Creator
Book design and production Thaïs Lips
Editing Thaïs Lips and Spencer Thomason, Ph.D
Published by Translations Decoder LLC
Centennial, CO, USA 2015

www.translationsdecoder.com
ISBN-13: 978-0996956307
(My Spiritual Life)
ISBN-10: 0996956301
All rights reserved

This book was translated and adapted from Iris Fróes, *A Imitação do Menino Jesus*, 1935, Rio de Janeiro, Brazil, 1st edition. All Brazilian editions of this book received a Roman Catholic Church *Nihil Obstat.*

Disclaimer

This book is meant to supplement, not replace, the Roman Catholic Catechism. The publisher advises parents and educators to take full responsibility orienting children for their understanding and to knowing their limits. Before practicing the skills described in this book, be sure that children do not take risks beyond their experience, aptitude, training, mental and emotional comfort level.

Although the publisher has made every effort to ensure that the information in this book was correct at press time, the publisher does not assume and hereby disclaims any liability to any party for any loss, damage, or disruption caused by errors, omissions, or interpretations, regardless of cause.

Author Iris Fróes
1902 – 1975
Brazilian writer, poet and journalist.

Translator Thaïs Lips

Thaïs, the granddaughter of author Iris Fróes, is an English, Portuguese, French, and Spanish translator. She attended law school in Brazil, has a Certificate of Proficiency in English from the University of Michigan, and a Teaching English as a Second Language certificate from the University of Colorado in Denver. She lives in Denver, CO, where she is currently the president of the Colorado Translators Association. She has lived in Brazil, England, Wales, France, and Oman.

Acknowledgment

Dr. Spencer Thomason, my dearest friend Gus, an early childhood educator, among other things, who helped me to make my grandmother's work a reality in the 21st century.

www.ingramcontent.com/pod-product-compliance
Lightning Source LLC
LaVergne TN
LVHW010026070426
835510LV00001B/7